Ancient Greece

STREAMS OF HISTORY SERIES

BY *Ellwood Wadsworth Kemp*

Ancient Greece

Table of Contents

The Geography of Greece

Earlier in our history work we studied the geography of four countries. Two of them—Egypt and Babylon—were large and in rich valleys; the other two—Palestine and Phœnicia—were small, had rather thin soil, were cut up by hills and mountains, and had no great rivers in them.

In the two great river countries, the people could sail up the rivers, which ran from one end of the country to the other, and then float back on the current. By this means everybody in the country came to know one another somewhat, and to have much the same ways of thinking and living; and so it was easy for them also to have just one ruler, or king.

But in the small countries we studied,—Palestine and Phœnicia,—which were so cut up by rugged mountains, and had no great rivers running through them, we found it was hard for the people to have just one person to rule them. They were much more likely to break up into small groups of people, each having its own customs and ways of life as well as its own ruler. It was so most of the time in Palestine, and almost always so in Phœnicia, except that sometimes a great king, like Hiram, might rule in Tyre, and have a loose control over the other great cities in the country.

Now all these people whom we have been studying about,—the Babylonians, the Egyptians, and the Jews,—when they grew rich, traded what they had to sell to the Phœnicians; and the Phœnicians, brave people that they were, went out all over the Mediterranean and traded with all the peoples living on its borders,—not only taking them wheat, barley, dyes and fruits, but also taking many beautiful and useful things, such as tools and vessels for farm and household. They also taught them the alphabet, which the Eastern countries had worked out by patient thought and labor of several thousand years.

One of the very first countries to which the Phœnicians came, in going westward, was the land of the Greeks. It would take them but five or six days to go from their own country to Greece in one of the boats which we studied about in the first volume of this series, and not even so long as that for them to reach one of the many beautiful green islands which lay between their country and Greece.

Now, since we are about to study the Greek people, I want you to see something of the country in which they lived.

If we could have taken one of those triremes with a Phœnician trader and gone with him on a trading trip to Greece, we would have first noticed, as we came within forty or fifty or seventy-five miles of the country, a great many islands out in the sea, looking just like stepping-stones to tempt people into the Greek coast, and to tempt the Greek people, who lived on the coast, out to trade with the people around; and as we went on up to the coast of Greece, we would see ever so many arms of the sea creeping far up into the country, making excellent landing places for boats,—just the kind of places to get easily what the people had to sell, and to trade off to them the things in the boat. And it was a fact also that the many islands, scattered out in the sea right in the face of Greece, had nearly every one of them good harbors. It was also true that the arms of the sea ran far up into the mainland of Greece, making, all told, so many excellent harbors, that the peoples around the Mediterranean easily learned to trade with Greece. And the Greeks, on the other hand, became active and daring, and traveled much around the Mediterranean, trading with everybody and planting colonies wherever a favorable trading spot was found.

But another most striking thing we would have noticed as we approached the country on the boat, would have been that Greece looked like a mountain rising straight out of the blue

Mediterranean. When we were far off, it would have looked like one solid mountain; but as we came nearer, say eight or ten miles away, we should have thought Greece was nothing but mountain peaks and crags.

The fact is, it was somewhat more than mountain peaks, but not so very much more. To begin with, the whole country was somewhat smaller than Indiana. It was a part of Europe, but its size on the map as compared to the rest of Europe was about the size of the little finger nail as compared to the size of the palm of the hand; and as compared with the size of Asia, it would compare about as the size of Rhode Island would with the whole of North America.

But now as to the mountains. There is almost in the center of Greece a high mountain called Par-nas'sus. It is a beautiful mountain, and persons can climb it. We will imagine ourselves on top of it, to get a look over Greece. In every direction we would look, we would see mountains; and not very regular ones, either, but often knotted and twisted ones running in all directions, and of every shape; then, again, in another direction would be a long ridge of mountains like a backbone, and running off from it ever so many spurs, like ribs. As we stood on top of Parnassus and looked around, it would seem like a vast, wild, rugged country. The cliffs and crags would be steep and barren; there would be but few roads leading over them on account of their steepness.

But as we looked down toward the feet of these rugged cliffs, we would see scattered all about among them little plains and upland hollows. The very largest of the plains would be perhaps as large as a good-sized county; then some would be as large as a township; others would be smaller, not larger than a good-sized farm; and some would be mere tiny patches in a hollow between two mountains, perhaps not larger than a good-sized field.

Now one thing that came about from having Greece cut up into so many pieces, and with such high mountain walls around them, was that hundreds of little cities, or villages, as we would often call them, grew up all over the country, each having its own customs and ways of living, and each its own form of government. You see the mountains were so high and so steep, and so few paths or roads lead from one side to the other, that the people living on the two sides could not become well acquainted with each other. They grew up not caring much for any Greek people except those living in their own little valley. When they did meet others, it would be to fight them for some little trouble or other which might arise, or simply because they were jealous of their growth. If you would imagine each one of the principal cities of your own state ruling itself entirely, and making all its laws, and fighting the other cities much of the time, it would be much like it was in Greece.

Another thing which made this trouble all the worse was the rivers. Greece had no large river running all through it from end to end, like the Nile in Egypt or the Mississippi in our own country. There were several small rivers in the country, but the mountains were so steep and so near the shore that it made the rivers very rapid, short and often rocky. There was not a single river in all Greece upon which one could travel with a boat. In winter and spring, when it rained and the snow melted off the mountains, the rivers would plunge down the mountain side and with terrible strength overflow the meadows (no wonder the Greeks made their river-gods having bodies of strong beasts); then in the summer time they would be entirely dry. Thus the rivers did not make natural roadways from one part of the country to another; and this helped, like the mountains, to keep the people separated, and caused each small group to build up a little city-state by itself and to care very little for any of the other city-states. For these reasons you can partly see why it was not easy for Greece, in all the thousand years her little snarling city-states were growing up, to have just one united state and one ruler over them all, as we have in the United States.

But there was another thing about this rugged country of which I have been telling you, that was much to the advantage of the Greeks. It helped them to defend their country from enemies. There were very few passes in the mountains, and often the mountains would come right down to the water's edge and against those arms of the sea I told you about, so that there would just be room for a wagon to crawl between the sea and the steep cliff. Now, if enemies tried to come from the north down into the country and capture the Greeks, a few brave men could so completely guard these passes that they could keep back a whole army. In one of these passes Leonidas, the Spartan king, and his brave handful of men guarded the pass of Ther-mop'-y-lae and kept back for several days the whole Persian army of hundreds of thousands of men.

If the Greeks had not been so selfish and had been willing to help one another when the enemies tried to get into their country to conquer them, they could have so completely stopped up these passes and narrow paths as to make it almost impossible for an enemy to conquer them. It was a pity the Greeks never could learn to work together—not even in time of greatest danger.

There were several other ways in which the mountains had an influence on the lives of the Greeks: in the first place, they made the soil often rather stony and thin, for fully five-sixths of the country was so barren and rocky that it was fit only for pasture; and although there were rich spots in places, yet what the Greeks got from the soil they had to work for; this made them self-reliant, hardy and full of health, and this was good for them. It is not necessarily the country where the soil is exceedingly rich and people have to work but little for a living that has the strongest and wisest men. Then another way the mountains influenced the people, was in their religion. Some of the peaks were high and covered almost all year with snow. This was especially true of Mt. Olympus, up in the northeastern part of Greece. On the top of this snow-capped, cloud-capped mountain, to which they could not climb, the Greeks imagined their chief gods and goddesses lived. Far up in the snows and clouds they had their homes, and only occasionally came down from the top to mingle with the people below. These mountains were clothed at their feet and far up their sides with groves of beech, ash, pine and oak. The Greeks imagined also that far above in their upland hollows in the forests, in caverns and in quiet places of retreat, many gods and goddesses dwelt. In these groves and grottoes priestesses lived, and listened to the murmuring leaves of the oaks or breathed in the vapors which came from the cavern, and thus tried to find out the way the gods wished them to act. These places where they would go to consult their gods were called *oracles*. A very famous one, where Zeus was consulted, was at Dodona in an oak grove in Epirus, in northwestern Greece, but the most famous in all Greece was the Oracle of Delphi, up on the slope of a mountain adjoining Mt. Parnassus, in a cavern from which a vapor came. There was a steep cliff immediately above, and a great chasm below. Here the richest temple of all Greece was built by the money paid by those who came to consult the oracle and worship Apollo.

The mountains also furnish fine stone for building, especially a blue and green stone called porphyry; and a very beautiful marble, which they used for making statues, as fine as the world has ever seen. There were silver, iron and copper in the mountains, and these helped in their commerce by giving them something of which to coin money, and likewise something to sell. They also furnished them material for making useful tools for farm and household.

In the forests of the mountains, plains and fields, were many animals, both tame and wild, which were used for food. The wild boar, deer, wolf and bear for large game, and the quails, hares, thrushes, partridges, pigeons, for small, gave food for the table and enabled the Greeks to enjoy the delights of hunting.

The temperature of Greece was neither very cold nor very hot; the atmosphere was dry and bright; the breezes came in everywhere from the mountains and the sea, to cool and refresh; for there was no spot in all Greece more than fifteen miles from a mountain or forty miles from the sea: all this tended to make the Greek quick and energetic. In such a climate he could work, take gymnastic exercises,—often without any clothing, and never with much,—participate with delight in the festivals to the gods, and enjoy the chase in the forest and field.

Thus we see that notwithstanding the Greek lived in a little country, cut up by mountains very greatly, and with rather a thin soil, yet take it all in all—mountain, wood, cliff, rock, sea, river, sky, island and ocean, all beautifully combined -it was a delightful and invigorating earth and sky which surrounded him, and stimulated him to produce the rarest grace and beauty in art ever produced by any people in the world. And in the festivals which he enjoyed, with music, song and dance; in the worship of the gods and goddesses; in stately processions; and in their games which gathered together all that would delight both body and mind, they lived almost as if their life was one continual holiday. The Greek's ideal was a beautiful soul in a beautiful body. His beautiful country no doubt greatly aided and stimulated him, as we have seen, to think much about and to work out this ideal.

Greece in Her Infancy or the Time of Homer

"WE will travel today Harold," said the teacher, "with our imagination, not to the river Nile nor to the Phœnician land with its ships, but to Greece, a little country far to the east, jutting out from the southern coast of Europe into the Mediterranean Sea, and looking like a hand with stubby little fingers. This country is four or five days' travel by trireme from Egypt,—Kufu's country,—which we studied about in the first volume of this series; and five or six days' travel in a Phœnician boat westward would have brought us to its green islands and lovely shores. I want to tell you about this country when it was very young and but few people were living in it. We will first see it when it is a mere infant, as it were, and afterward see it grow to be a man." Harold closed his eyes to imagine the sea, mountains, valleys and rivers, and when he opened them again he found himself alone in the loveliest valley he had ever seen. Behind him lay the sea; to the right were hills crowned with tall pine trees; on the left was a thick wood, and beyond it the blue mountain peaks touched the blue sky. Harold stopped to pick up a few acorn cups and knock a prickly green chestnut bur from the tree.

He wandered on and presently was much surprised to see a stone wall a short distance before him. He walked in at the open gate. It was nearly dark by this time, and he did not know whether he was in a house or a barn, for he heard sounds of both animals and men; but being very tired, he lay down on one of the benches of polished stone just inside the gate and slept soundly until morning. He found his neighbors were awake, too. There were cows, a watchdog, sheep, goats, and pigs in their pens, built around the inside of the square wall; and there, too, were the rooms for the men who tended them, and rooms for the women who milked the cows and goats.

At one end of this court was a long portico with columns, which was the entrance to the real house. Harold thought he was never in such an odd-looking front yard.

A little boy of Harold's size came and stood by the side of one of the columns. He was barefoot and wore a garment thrown loosely over the shoulders, for Greece was so warm that only on colder days and near the mountains did one need much clothing. Harold joined Phœnix (for that was the boy's name), and after saying a pleasant good morning to a stranger who was folding up his bed of skins in the portico, he said, "Come with me into the doma (that was what he called the dwelling room) and I will ask my father if you may stay with me."

They passed through a dark hall into a very large open room, where there were many men, and were soon at the side of a kind-faced man, who said he would be glad to have his little son's guest remain with him. He was a tall, straight man, and his light yellow hair was arranged in long curls. He wore over his chiton (for so Phœnix called his dress) a beautiful red cloak. It was not a cloak such as we know, but a large square piece of cloth beautifully embroidered around the edge, draped about the body and fastened on the left shoulder with a silver clasp.

Harold sat on a footstool and looked about him. In two rows on either side of the room were wooden columns which held up the roof. Near the center of the room was a large column, and leaning against it were a great number of spears, which Phœnix said would be used to attack their enemies on the other side of the mountains. At one side of the room was a fireplace built of brick. There was no chimney, but Harold did not mind the smoke, for he was eager to see what was being prepared for breakfast. Two slave women, who were captives from another valley, cooked the meat. They put pieces of beef on iron sticks and slowly roasted it over the open fire. A young girl lifted a copper kettle from the crane and stirred something that very much resembled oatmeal.

Many men were in the room. Phœnix explained that some of these were his older brothers, who were married, and who, with their families, had rooms in another part of the house, while others were guests and strangers, who sat on the hearth-stone and sought his father's protection.

"Come, Phœnix, and take my shield to the room above," said the largest and strongest of them all. It took both boys to carry it to the apartment over the doma. There were so many interesting shields, swords, helmets, greaves and spears, besides the household goods stowed away, that Harold wished to look at them all. He was given one of the prettiest chairs to use for his own while he was there. It had a curved back all in one piece of wood, with a carved border, and with a bronze horse embedded in the center. It was a comfortable chair, although it had neither rockers nor arms. "What a fine store I could have, if all these things were mine," thought Harold.

When they came down, the door of the doma was opened, and there stood a gentle woman with a fine face, dressed in a long white chiton. She bade her son come to his breakfast. Harold followed, and when all the children were seated, a little table was set before each one. Harold enjoyed his wholesome breakfast of goat's milk and barley bread, and was too polite to seem to notice the very odd but beautifully shaped spoon and bowl given him. After breakfast they went to the large garden back of the house, where Phœnix proudly pointed out his own special young apple trees, which were bearing for the first time, the trim rows of asters and the abundant crop of beans which he had been taught to care for during the summer. Near by was a goose pond where Penelope, Phœnix's sister, was throwing bread to the geese.

She presently came to them, and they entered the house together—not the room where they first went, but the one back of

13

that, where Harold and the others ate breakfast, the thalium, or women's room, as it was called. There sat the mother and the sisters of Phœnix, sewing. The mother passed from one to the other, showing one how to turn a hem and another how to arrange the colors on the border she was embroidering. Even little Penelope was taking stitches in a chiton which was intended for her brother's birthday, for all girls among the early Greeks learned to sew and spin and to do all kinds of household work. Harold could not decide which was the prettiest of Phœnix's four older sisters, for they were all beautiful; but he liked Narcissa, the one with golden hair, the best, for she was the most gentle. A dark-haired little girl, not much older than Penelope, carried Narcissa's silk to her, arranged her footstool, and brought her a drink. She did not look happy, and Harold saw her wipe away the tears as she gazed toward the sea; for she remembered how, not many months ago, she was stolen from her country and brought by the Phœnician and sold to be a sewing-maid in this household. Narcissa found her weeping, and kissed her softly. Harold wondered if she would ever forget her home, and the parents and brothers and sisters from whom she had been stolen.

At dinner time the work was put away, the hunters returned, bringing a large stag, and men and women sat down in the doma. The slaves brought in jugs of wine and cases of water, and these the master mixed in an earthen urn of the most beautiful pattern. Its handles were traced with gold, and a silver dove perched on each. Small tables were brought in, and after being carefully washed, were placed, one before each person, for the Greeks never all sat at one table to dine as we do. The kettle of peas was lifted from the crane and then put into small dishes that looked like the saucers Harold had seen under his mother's flower-pots, only they were not so well shaped. The roasted pork and beef were carried to the table of the carvers, and there cut into small pieces before being served. Baskets of onions were passed around, and barley and wheat bread looked very tempting in baskets of golden wire. A piece of cheese, a cup of olive oil, and a bronze saucer of honey completed the food they would have for dinner. Before any one ate, a slave poured water from a golden pitcher into a basin, and each washed his hands; for since there were no forks, and spoons were little used, the fingers needed to be quite clean. Instead of using napkins they cleaned their fingers, after the meal, on pieces of dough. They drank wine, but it was well mixed with water, and the Greek was so temperate in its use that he rarely became intoxicated.

After the tables were removed and the crumbs picked up off the floor, the father took his place on a great throne-like seat covered with a fine rug. Here he sat with the other people grouped around. On one side Harold noticed a platform up high, much like the band stand he saw in town. Here musicians sat and played upon the harps and sang the songs of the heroes— among others a song about the capture of the Golden Fleece. "This is very beautiful," said Harold. "Oh, wait until we go to the market place and hear Homer," said Phœnix. "I will ask my father if we may go with him."

Just then a bugle sounded, and both boys scampered away to the outer wall. Coming over the ridge beyond the meadow, was a drove of white oxen with glistening coats, accompanied by their driver and his servants. Phœnix clapped his hands at first, but, thinking again, said, "I hope it isn't Narcissa he is coming for." The man proudly approached the wall, and entering the doma was presented at the throne of the chief. The next day when he went away he took Narcissa to be his wife and left the oxen, for they were the price her father received for her. Narcissa rode a pretty gray horse as she went away. The dark-haired little slave girl whom she took with her smiled back from the donkey-wagon that held the beautiful and useful garments Narcissa and her maidens had woven.

One morning, just after breakfast, the father with several of his sons and slaves walked out into the country to oversee the men who farmed his land. The men who tended the land lived in rude but

15

well-kept huts. The father went to the threshing floor, where they saw a servant driving a pair of oxen over the barley. Phœnix and Harold gathered up what was thrown to the side, for Phœnix might have this for his own planting. Harold became interested in a man who was using a pick to break up the ground, for the plows drawn by oxen were not much better than sharpened sticks and did not loosen the ground well. Laertes (for that was his name) spoke kindly to Harold, and pointed out his hut among the rest. He explained that the little bunch of wool which Harold noticed on Laertes' door told that a little girl baby had come to live in his home. He pointed out for Harold the road to the vineyards where the grapes were ripening, and let him pet the sheep whose coats were so carefully kept. The chariot of a nobleman, with four horses hitched abreast, passed by to the race-course; a soothsayer came muttering something about the flight of a flock of crows meaning bad luck to the olive crop; a traveler sat down to tie the cord of his sandal. The goats came up from the meadows, and the maidens came with earthen jars to milk them. Harold had had a lovely day in the country, but it was now evening and he bade farewell to Laertes and returned with the others to the town; for although he had been so interested in the home of Phœnix that he had not noticed other houses, he was really in a small city just beginning to grow up in a beautiful valley, for at this time in Greece there were many little independent towns. The houses in each town were far apart, and many families often lived in each one.

Early the next morning the men made ready to go to the market place. There, after seeing the onions, olives, fruits, beans and melons sold, they gathered in groups around the porticoes of the market place, and the boys listened to a heated discussion of the question of waging war against a neighboring valley. Among the people Harold noticed Laertes in his coat of lion skin and asked him what he was going to say; but Phœnix quickly drew Harold aside and said that Laertes would not be allowed to speak, for he was only a laborer, and that his father and brothers and others who were noblemen would decide what wars should be waged. Just then the soothsayer whom Harold had seen that day at the farm appeared. Taking a scepter in his hands as a sign of authority, he began to speak. He said he had dreamed of a returning army and many captives, fair women and strong men, of shields and plundered gold. All listened attentively, and it was decided to make war on a neighboring city, chiefly because they were jealous of its growth, for the people of the city had given no offense. Phœnix loved to hear of war, and said that when he was a man he would go with war-chariots to every valley and make the chiefs give up their gold and silver, that he would bring home their men and women as slaves, that he would gain the laurel crown in the race-course, and then he would be the greatest man in all Greece.

Presently there appeared in the market place a man with head slightly bent forward, with cautious step and intent face, who put his hands before him, and finding his harp, drew it to him. As his fingers moved gently over the strings, a deep silence fell all around him—it was Homer, the blind poet. "How delightful!" whispered Phœnix; "he is going to sing more about the beautiful Helen and the siege of Troy. About Achilles, the brave boy-hero, and Ajax the powerful, and wise old Nestor, and the wooden horse. We must listen, for he cannot be with us many years, and he who listens best now can best tell his sons the story. My father says many traditions have been lost because no one remembered them well enough to tell them to his sons." Harold thought they would remember because the story was so beautiful and so beautifully sung. Homer told only a part that day, and at evening the boys repeated at home parts of what they had heard.

While Phœnix was taking his lesson in music from one of the captive princes, and learning to repeat legends and wise sayings after a trusted slave, Harold stole away and watched the older boys and men at their contests in running and leaping. They had all been

17

trained to be great athletes, and even the poorest seemed to Harold to be very good. They all did so well he wished everybody could be awarded an olive branch, which was given only to the victor.

He liked to play with Phœnix's little cart, and many a game of marbles and checkers they enjoyed together, while Penelope stood by with her kitten in her arms and Phœnix's little dog bit at the marbles.

Seated after play on his beautifully shaped chair, he never tired of looking at the furniture of the doma. There were chairs, and wooden chests with ivory figures on the lids, couches, carpets and rugs, all of which had been made by hand. Near the hearth on the floor and hanging on the wall were all varieties of earthenware vessels and kettles of copper and bronze, for the Phœnicians had taught the Greeks how to make all these things. A large red earthenware vase was placed near the cupboard where the goblets stood. This vase was the prettiest in the room. It had around its top a picture of a hunter and his dogs—done in black. The figures looked rather stiff, but they were pretty, considering they had to be cut in the vase and then filled with black paint. The greatest beauty was in the shape of the vase, and in the handles, which were large and symmetrical. On the walls were great plates of brass ornamented with iron. On the great one that hung over the door to the thalium was the picture of a tower over the city wall. A woman, tall and graceful, stood there with a little baby in her arms. She was looking beseechingly into the face of a young warrior clad in armor from head to foot. Just showing beyond the wall on a hill was the army to which he seemed about to return. Harold looked so often at this picture that he would never forget it. There were many other pictures, and all interesting, and, like other pictures of ancient times, all made of metals. It is thought by many that at this time the Greeks had not yet learned to paint pictures.

On the day that the men were to start out to battle, all assembled in the doma and prepared to offer a sacrifice to Ares, the god of war. A strong ox, with a wreath of flowers around its neck, was led in and killed before the hearth. Part of it was put upon the hearth, which was their altar, and burned. By the manner of burning and the color of the smoke, the oracles tried to tell what would be the result of the battle. Prayers were made to Ares, and in the thalium sacrifice was offered to Hestia, the goddess of the hearth, and prayers were offered that she might protect the household. Then the men, clad in armor, with bows and arrows, and slings, and spears, and shields, marched away a few miles across the mountains to fight a neighboring city; for, as I told you, one thing the Greek cities never could learn was to be friends with one another.

But Harold and Phœnix remained at home, passing many days playing marbles, jack-stones and ball, very much as boys do now, till one morning several ox carts were drawn up before the outer gate and Phœnix and Harold were delighted when they were told they might go with a farm hand on a journey to the seashore to trade with the Phœnicians. In the first cart was placed the fine linen and woolen goods that Phœnix's mother and sisters had woven. In another was wool, and in another the finest of the olives that Laertes had brought in from the farm. Hirus, the brother of the dark-haired little slave girl, drove the oxen for Phœnix. As they lay that night on the soft wool, near the seashore, and looked up at the clear sky and the stars, Phœnix told Harold about the ships and the trade of the Phœnicians; and in the quiet night, after Phœnix was asleep, Hirus told Harold how he and his Phœnician kinsmen had once on the sea been taken captive and sold to Phœnix's father. He said they did the finest carving and work in metals, and that the Greeks were just beginning to learn to do that kind of work. Harold at last fell asleep listening to the dark-eyed slave's stories of the wonderful work of his people—of how other kings hired them to build their temples, of how they braved the roughest sea to get tin from distant lands, and of the rich palaces of their kings. The next morning they were busy trading at the coast. The Phœnicians were there in their ships, and everybody was busy. Phœnix traded the wool plucked from his own sheep for a silver cup. When the wagons went back the next day, they were loaded with shields and spears, chairs, tapestries and rugs from the countries about Babylon; jewels and wheat from Egypt, and purple dyes, cashmere shawls and metal looking-glasses from the land of Phœnicia. Thus Harold saw how the beautiful little country of Greece learned many of its first lessons about useful and beautiful things by trading with the Phœnicians, and how the Phœnicians gathered together the things made in the countries we studied about earlier—Egypt, Palestine and Babylon—and brought them westward and traded them to people who had not yet learned to make things so useful and beautiful.

By the Greeks learning all that the Phœnicians had to teach them about the alphabet, about weights and measures, about purple dye for making hangings for palaces, and robes for kings, about how to tan skins by using the root of the evergreen oak of Greece, and how to make useful things of iron, copper and silver, they became more than the simple farmers which Harold saw as he took his trip through the country; for they soon learned to make ships like those which the Phœnicians used, and after a time became the greatest traders on the Mediterranean Sea.

But although the Greeks at this early time were very simple and plain, yet at this very time they wrote a book, which people read with as much delight now as they did thousands of years ago. It is one of the greatest books ever written, telling us most of what we now know of early Greece, with her brave heroes and beautiful women. The book is made up of the songs of Homer, and it is called the "Iliad." Readers continue to enjoy this book in our own day, and in this way, although Greece died thousands of years ago, the best things the Greeks wrote still live as fresh as ever in the life of every good scholar.

The Youth of Greece and Her Struggles for Liberty

PHIDIPPIDES started swiftly from Athens, "over the hills and under the dales, down pits and up peaks," reaching Sparta, a hundred and fifty miles away, in less than two days. His country was in danger, and there was not a moment to be lost. He went to ask help of the Spartans, for word had come to Athens that the Persian king, Darius, was moving straight toward the beautiful city to destroy her; and to meet Persia, Athens would need Sparta's aid. You wonder why this great king was coming over to Greece? He was angry with the Athenians, and I will tell you why.

It was now a long time, four or five hundred years, since Homer lived, and Greece had changed in many ways. It had grown much richer, and there were now the new poets Sappho and Hesiod, and many sculptors, who made beautiful statues to represent the gods and goddesses, and ornamented the graceful Greek temples.

Every five years the people from all Greece gathered to see the Olympic games, which were held in honor of their god, Zeus. There the young men and boys jumped, ran and wrestled with one another, and those who did best received a laurel crown. The boys who won were very proud of their crowns. It was at the games that the poets recited their new poems. Do you think that by gathering together in this way the people would understand each other better and be willing to help one another when they got into difficulty, as Athens is now?

You remember that, in Homer's time, there were little city-states scattered about in Greece separated by the hills and mountains. Well, these villages have now grown into towns and there are many more of them than in Homer's time. The people still do not live together in one government as they should, if they wish to be strong, but perhaps when Darius comes to fight Athens they will forget their little jealousies of one another and will join to protect their beautiful land. Sometimes, when these cities became crowded or the people disliked their king, they left their home-city, and sailed away as colonists to build new homes in Italy, Sicily, and far across the Ægean Sea along the coast of Asia Minor. Now, it is about something these cities in Asia Minor did that Darius, the Persian king, is angry. You do not now quite see why, but I think you will presently. But first I must tell you another thing that was changed since Homer's time. There were no longer kings in the little states ruling the people, except at Sparta, which was the largest city in southern Greece; and this king had men called ephors to help him. At Athens, the chief city in Attica, there had been no king for a long time. Long ago the people had grown tired of having one man rule them, and had chosen men called archons, and legislators, to rule them and make their laws.

Solon was one of the wisest of these men. He had traveled in many lands, in Egypt and Asia, was of noble birth, and kind to all the people. The rich had gotten most of the power in their hands and left the poor unprotected, but when Solon was chosen to be both archon and legislator, he made new laws to help the common people. They were glad of this, but because he did not divide the lands again as had been done before and give them a share, they were dissatisfied. But Solon saw that the people were better off than before, and hoping that they would stay so, he went away from Athens to travel again, spending, it is said, two years in travel and study—in the wiser and richer countries of the Old East.

Sometimes in the cities of this little land of Greece a nobleman who had been disappointed in not getting some office which he wanted, or who did not like the ruler, would say to the people, that if they would help him to put down the rightful ruler of the country so that he himself might rule, he would help all the people to have an easier time. A man who got the power this way was called a tyrant. I want to tell you about the tyrant Pisistratus, who seized the power after Solon went away.

Pisistratus came hurriedly driving into Athens one day, covered with blood and his mules bleeding. He told the people that his enemies had tried to kill him because he was the people's friend. This pleased the people, and they voted him a bodyguard of soldiers. With these he gained control of Athens and ruled for many years. He was a good ruler and did much to improve Athens. He built the Academy, which was something like the beautiful parks in some of our cities, and made a fine gymnasium in it, for the boys to exercise in. He also built a temple to Athena on the Acropolis,—a great rocky hill in the center of Athens.

But after him came his two sons, and they were not so good as their father. One of them was killed, and the other, Hippias, was driven out of the country. He went to the Persian court, but we shall presently see that he came back to Greece. After Hippias, there was one more friend of the people, Cleisthenes, who did much to help Athens by giving her better laws. After him the people were ruled again by archons, and it is at this time, 490 years before Christ was born, that Phidippides ran quickly to Sparta to ask help against the Persians.

The Grecian cities on the coast of Asia Minor had been ruled for several years by the Persian king, Cyrus, who was a great and good ruler of the Persians; but a few years before this time Cyrus died, and Darius came to be the ruler. Before the Persians conquered the Greek cities in Asia Minor, these cities had been ruled by Croesus of Lydia, the little country just east of them. He was kind to them, but the Persians, who liked to conquer all the countries about them, not only made the Greeks pay much money to them, but they had to be the Persian king's soldiers as well. Men who loved to rule themselves as dearly as the Greeks would not like this.

Darius, who now ruled over Persia, reaching from the Indus River to the Ægean Sea, found it so large that he needed many men to help him govern it. Many of the people over whom he ruled were not at all like the real Persians, but lived and dressed very differently. Darius did not care for this, as all he wanted was that they should pay him money and fight his battles. Would these men make as good soldiers as the Greeks, do you think?

Not long before Phidippides went to Sparta, the Grecian cities in Asia Minor which Darius ruled had revolted, and asking help of Athens and Eretria, their near kinsmen, they had together burned Sardis, one of Darius' richest and finest cities in Asia Minor. This was why Darius was so angry with Athens. He soon punished the colonies on the coast, and then shot an arrow toward Athens, to show that he meant to punish her next, but lest he forget (for he had many things to do in his great empire), he had a slave say to him each day at dinner, "Master, remember the Athenians"; and now he was getting ready to remember them. He had sent heralds to the different Grecian cities, bidding them send him "earth and water" as a sign that they would serve him. Most of the states had done so, but Athens had thrown the herald who came to her into a pit, and Sparta had thrown hers into a well. You may be sure a great king, ruling a vast empire, would feel very angry to have a little country like Greece treat his messengers in this way.

When his army was ready, he sent it across the Ægean Sea, toward Athens. As soon as Athens heard that the Persians were coming she sent Phidippides, the fleet-footed, as I have already told you, to Sparta for help; but Sparta could send no aid because the moon was not yet full, and it was against her law to start to battle before the full moon; so Athens was left to meet the enemy alone, but she did it bravely.

When the Persians reached Greece and landed at Marathon, led by the traitor Hippias (you remember who he was, do you not?), they found a little army of the Athenians gathered upon the hillside back of Marathon, eighteen or twenty miles northeast of Athens, under the Athenian general, Miltiades, ready to meet them. Without waiting for the Persians to begin the attack, the Athenians, singing, rushed down into the plain on the enemy so furiously that the Persians became frightened and confused, but not so the Greeks, who fought until the Persians turned and fled to their ships. The Greeks followed and destroyed many as they tried to get into their boats. One brave Greek seized a boat and held it fast till his hand was cut off.

Marathon was a great victory, and the Athenians were very proud of it. Just as the battle was over, the Spartans came up, but they were too late to help drive the Persians away. The Athenians had fought the great battle almost alone, and in after years the thought of it led them to do just as great things.

Miltiades did not let his victorious army camp on the battlefield that night and enjoy a feast of the many good things which the Persians left, but marched his soldiers across the country eighteen miles, without a halt, back to Athens. He thought that the Persians would next try to capture the city. The tired soldiers had only just reached home when they saw the Persians sail into the bay near Athens; but when the enemy saw the same brave men who had the day before defeated them, ready to fight again, they sailed away to their own country in Asia as fast as they could.

After the Persians were gone, Miltiades had the brazen arms and shields which had been captured from them melted and made into a statue of the goddess Athena and placed on the Acropolis. Darius was so sure that he could defeat the Greeks that he had brought a great block of marble along to put up in the city as a monument to celebrate his victory; but it was used for a different purpose, for Phidias, the great Grecian sculptor, made a beautiful statue from it.

The Athenians thought they had driven the Persians away forever, but there was one wise man in Greece—Themistocles—

who did not think so. He thought that they would come again, so he urged the Athenians to build a great many new ships by taxing themselves and from the money of their gold mines, for there were excellent gold mines near Athens. Another wise and good man, called Aristides, thought they did not need any more ships and that it would be better to give the money to the people. Some of the people thought as Aristides, and others wanted to have the ships built. At last they saw that one of the men, in order to keep peace in the little Athenian state, must be sent away; so all the people gathered in Athens one day, and each wrote on a shell the name of the man he wished to send away. When they counted the names, it was found that there were six thousand shells for Aristides, which meant that he must leave his home and go into another country. This was called *ostracism*. It took this name from the name of the shell, or tablet, upon which the vote was written. Themistocles then went on building the ships until the Greeks had a large fleet.

While the Greeks were building their ships, Darius was getting another army ready to come back to Greece. He was so certain he could conquer the Greeks that he was going to try again.

You see he did not know that, even if there were not many Greeks, they were very brave and had been well trained for war. He did not know what excellent training the Greeks obtained in their gymnasiums at Athens and how the Spartan boys by severe training, gathering reeds for their own rough beds, hunting on the mountains, eating coarse food and having to go barefoot winter and summer, became the best soldiers of the world in their time. The Spartan women, too, were often as brave as the men. They said to their sons, "Bring home your shield or come home on it," which meant that they must never give up to the enemy. They must either conquer him or die fighting him. The Athenians did not train their children to fight quite so well as Sparta did, but they knew how to make good plans to capture the enemy. Would these Grecians who ruled themselves and loved their homes and children, their little farms and gods, fight better than the Persian soldiers, who were hired to fight, and fought only for the king?

Darius had gathered together only part of the second army with which he meant to conquer Greece when he died, and his son Xerxes took his place. Xerxes did not want to fight the Greeks, but his nobles wished him to do so; so, after great preparations, he concluded to lead the army himself.

In gathering together his army he sent heralds all over his vast country to tell the people to make ready for war. For eight long years he gathered together his soldiers, made armor and collected food, built roads and trained his men. Would not you think he could bring together a large army in eight years? When they were all gathered, they spent the winter in and about the city of Sardis in Asia Minor, which the Persians had built up again after the Greeks had burnt it.

Early in the spring 480 years before Christ, Xerxes started toward Greece with his great army, but it was a motley looking mass of men. The king rode in his chariot, which was drawn by eight white horses. In his gorgeous dress and chariot it must have been a beautiful sight. On either side of Xerxes were his best soldiers, the Immortals. Those who fought on foot wore coats of mail made of metal or quilted linen, which covered all the body except the head. They had also shields made of wicker-work, which were set in front of them, from behind which they shot with bow and arrow. Those who rode on horseback had coats of mail to cover the entire body, and these men carried a sword and knife for weapons. But besides the Immortals there were many who could not fight so well. Some were dressed in leopard skins and carried bows made of the ribs of palm leaves. Their arrows were reeds tipped with small, sharp stones, and some had only clubs with which to fight. Others had a lasso and long knife, while still others had short darts and knives. Some of the wilder tribes tried to protect their heads with wooden hats, but had no protection whatever for their bodies.

Xerxes, with his mighty army, marched westward across the country to the Hellespont, where he had had a bridge of boats built for his army to cross on. It took a long time for all the soldiers to cross, but at last they were all over and marched toward Greece.

While Xerxes was leading this part of his army around to the north, the Persian fleet had crossed the Ægean Sea to help him capture the Grecians.

When the Athenians heard that Xerxes was coming, they were filled with fear. Miltiades, who had led them at Marathon, was dead, and they did not know who could lead them to victory now. Finally they sent for Aristides, who, you remember, had been sent away by ostracism. Runners were sent from Athens all over Greece to ask aid of the different states, but nearly all the people were at the Olympic games. Finally the Spartans promised to send some soldiers to the narrow pass of Thermopylæ, which was a narrow road, just wide enough for a chariot to creep between the mountains and the sea, leading into central Greece. So Leonidas, with three hundred of the bravest Spartans and seven hundred Thespians, stationed himself there to meet the Persians.

Leonidas had not been at the pass long before Xerxes came. When Xerxes saw so few men, he sent a messenger to ask the Spartans to give up their arms. Leonidas sent him word to "come and take them." Then Leonidas and his men put on their finest armor, combed their long hair, and played at games in the sunshine. Xerxes thought the Greeks were crazy when he saw them combing their long hair, but a traitor Spartan in Xerxes' camp told him they always did so before a dangerous battle, and it did not mean they were careless but determined to fight to the last. Xerxes then sent some of his troops against them, but they had to fall back; this happened again and again, and perhaps Leonidas could have kept the Persians back until the rest of the Greeks returned from the games, had not a traitor gone to Xerxes and for money offered to show him a path which led over the mountains and behind Leonidas, who had placed only a few men to guard it.

Led by the traitor, the Persians came to the guards of the path, whom they soon killed, and then they marched down the mountain side toward Leonidas. It was yet early morning, and there was still time for all the Greeks to escape. Leonidas told his men that all might go except the Spartans. "We," said he, "must stay." Yet he knew that all who remained would be killed. The Thespians, who lived in a little city not far away, however, refused to go. They were brave, too. All day long this handful of men, clothed in brass from head to foot, and armed with spears, fought against the mighty Persian hosts, and at night not one of Leonidas' brave men was left. This, as I have told you, was just ten years after the battle of Marathon and four hundred and eighty years before the birth of Christ. It looked discouraging when the mighty Persian host marched through the pass and came on toward Athens. Do you think the Persians will now conquer Greece?

When the Persians had gained the victory at Thermopylæ, Xerxes, as I said, marched on toward Athens. The people of that city fled, and not knowing what to do they asked advice of their god, Apollo, at Delphi. The answer was, "The wooden walls will defend you and your children." The Greeks were not sure what this meant, but Themistocles said it meant for them to go into their ships, which you remember he had already persuaded the Athenians to build.

All the women and children were put on ships and sent away from Athens to the southern part of Greece; then the warriors made the rest of the ships ready to fight in the bay of Salamis. The people had just left the city when Xerxes marched into Athens and burned it. His ships had not helped him much yet, but he thought they could surely defeat the little Greek fleet which he saw in the bay of

Salamis, west of Athens, so he had a throne built on a mountain, not far from Salamis, that he might watch the battle.

The Greeks fought so bravely and so well that they cut the Persian fleet all to pieces. Xerxes became frightened, and taking most of his army, fled to Persia. He left quite a large number, however, in Greece, under his general, Mardonius; and not very long after, the Greeks fought another battle with him at Platæa. In this battle the Greeks were completely successful; and when Mardonius saw that he was defeated, he ran away with the men he had left, leaving great riches on the battlefield. The Greeks were glad to see him leave for Persia, for they thought that the Persians would never come again.

Thus, you see, this brave little country had defeated a country forty times as large, and by doing so prevented a king who cared nothing for common people from crushing out the liberty-loving Greeks. It made them very proud of themselves, and made them feel as if they could do great deeds. If the little city-states of Greece could now have been less selfish, and had all worked together, they might have done even more than they did. It was a pity they never could learn to work together. But even as it was, Athens now grew rapidly and did wonderful things, and of these things we will next study.

A Visit to Athens When Greece Was in Her Greatest Beauty

WHEN the Persians were at last driven away from Greece the people had time to look around and see what had been done to their country. Do you not think it must have been discouraging for them to come back and find their homes and temples all burned down? They must now begin all over and make a new city. It was surprising to see how quickly this was done.

One thing that helped them make Athens more beautiful than it had ever been before was this very war. Let me tell you how this was. All those cities in the AEgean Sea and in Asia Minor that we have spoken of were now free from Persia, but they were still afraid of the great Persian king. They thought Athens the strongest city of Greece, and wanted her to help them. So Athens and about two hundred of the cities around and in the AEgean Sea joined in a league, with Athens at the head. Another league was formed of the cities in southern Greece with Sparta at the head. Once a year men from each of these leagues met on the island of Delos to worship and to talk over important things about the union. If any of the cities had warships, they gave them to Athens to use; or if they had none, they gave money each year, and Athens built ships with it. This money was kept in Apollo's temple, on the island of Delos, and the temple grew very rich. But after a while Athens had as many ships as she thought she needed, and as the Persians did not come back again, she began to use this money to build up her own city. Thus you see how this war helped to make Athens more beautiful than she had ever been before. Besides making her people free and proud of their city, it gave them plenty of money to use.

I want to tell you now about a great man who lived in Athens at this time, and did more than any one else to make the city great and beautiful. His name was Pericles. He was a very handsome man, but that is not why we remember him. He was such a fine speaker that he generally made the Athenians believe what he said, and he easily led them to do what he wanted them to do. But even that is not the great thing. It is because he got them to do so many wise things and made Athens great as well as himself, that we remember him. Pericles had many wonderful buildings erected; some of them I want to tell you about. I wish I might take you there and let you see them all as they were. If we could really go to Athens, we could see only the ruins of many of them, and often only the places where some stood; for you must remember that Pericles has been dead more than two thousand years, and the beautiful buildings he had built are, many of them, crumbling to pieces, and some of them are entirely gone. Since we cannot see them, let us, with the help of what I can tell you from books I have read, try to get some idea of what Athens was like when Pericles lived.

You remember the Acropolis, of course, but you would hardly know it now. You must imagine it in the southwestern part of the city, a steep, high hill a thousand feet long and five hundred wide, with walls around the top to make it still steeper, so that no enemy could climb up the sides. Pericles had a flight of steps built up on the west side. They were seventy-one feet wide, rose by a gentle slope upward and were easy to climb. Let us imagine ourselves at the foot of these steps, ready to go up and look at Athens in all her beauty. Can you think how it would really seem to be there, with marble buildings and statues all around us? Now we will climb the steps, and when we come to the top we will pass into what they call a colonnade, which is much like a long path, bordered with beautiful columns and covered over; in fact, it was just two long rows of tall, beautiful columns holding up a roof. The gateways opening into this colonnade were called the Propylæa, and the

Greeks were very proud of them, for they formed most beautiful openings leading up to the doors of the temples.

After we pass through the Propylæa, we find ourselves on top of the Acropolis, facing the east, for we came up the west side. Almost in front of us is a great image of Athena, who, you remember, was Athens' best-loved goddess. This image, or statue, as it was called, was so tall that men far out at sea, miles away from Athens, could see it. It made the Athenians very happy to feel that Athena was thus watching over them and ready to help them. On our right hand, still facing east, was the most beautiful temple of Greece, and indeed, though there have been many greater ones, there has never been another one built in the world quite so graceful and pleasing. It was built in honor of and as the home of Athena, and was called the Parthenon. It was 226 feet long, 101 feet wide, and it took sixteen years to build it. A little distance away, it looks as if it were mostly rows of columns and not much building, but there are two large rooms, which are surrounded by the columns you see,—one is used in which to store the gold belonging to the Delian league of which I told you a little while ago. It is kept in Athens now, instead of at Delos. In the second room is one of the most beautiful statues that was ever made. You would know right away it was Athena, by her helmet and shield and the serpent coiled at her feet. It was made of ivory and gold, by Phidias, one of the very greatest artists of the world, who could carve marble or ivory into most beautiful shapes of men, women and animals. In many places on the Parthenon we can find Phidias' work. Here at the end, right under the roof, is some, and inside, clear around the rooms I told you of, is a broad strip of carved work which he did. Over on another part of the Acropolis is another very beautiful temple, called the Erechtheum, because it was built for the god Erechtheus. One odd as well as beautiful part of it was the porches, which instead of pillars to hold them up had figures of beautiful maidens carved in stone. We could stay a long time on the Acropolis, because, though not very large, it has a great many things to see; but let us pass again through the Propylæa, down the steps and into the city, for I want you to see some other wonderful things which Pericles gave to Athens.

You will be interested in what the boys of Athens are doing, so I will take you now to a gymnasium, for the Greeks loved a straight, healthy body quite as much as a beautiful building or statue. Pericles was one who believed that Athens needed strong, brave, perfect men, and the best way he knew to get them was to train together both the bodies and minds of the boys. So he did all he could to make their gymnasiums beautiful, and fitted them up with everything they needed in their exercises. They were all outside the city, so we will have to leave Athens to see them. All the Athenian boys are sent to the gymnasium as soon as they are old enough, and they spend the whole day, from sunrise to sunset, there. What do they all do there? I cannot begin to tell you all of it. They have teachers, who teach them the different exercises that are to make them strong and manly as well as beautiful; and the Greeks believed that to have a beautiful mind one must have also a beautiful body. They are stripped in the gymnasium of all their clothing, for the Athenian boys must learn to bear the hot sun or the cold winds without flinching; but you remember that the climate of Greece was generally very delightful, neither very cold nor very hot. In one part of the gymnasium is a race course, sprinkled several inches deep with loose sand, where the boys race with each other; not very easy work, do you think? The sand is put there on purpose to make it hard for them to run. In another place you see boys getting ready to wrestle; their bodies are oiled, then sprinkled over with fine sand, so they can hold each other better. This is rough work, but it exercises the whole body, and so is good for health and strength. We must not stop to see the other work now, but I may tell you that besides these exercises they are taught among others to box, throw the spear, jump, wrestle and run races.

But the Greeks did not like a man who could use only his body and not his mind, so they wanted their boys taught more than bodily exercise. All around three sides of the gymnasium were halls, with seats in them, where people could sit and talk. If you come with me to one of these halls, you will see one of the most interesting things in Greece, and I believe you will think it a fine kind of school. Here is a group of boys gathered around a man who is talking to them in a very plain, friendly way. Does that look like a school? Not much like our schools, you will say. Before we join the group I will tell you a little about the teacher, so you will understand better what they are doing. He is one of the men whom the Greeks call philosophers, which means *lovers of knowledge*. These men spend their lives trying to find out the truth about everything. They wish to know how the world came to be, what men ought to live for, and how a man should act in order that his life may be made best worth living. They meet the boys and young men and talk about these things with them. The boys ask them questions, and they answer the best they can, and ask questions of the boys in turn. These philosophers, especially those like the one I am going to tell you about, because they thought so much of simple life and were interested in common plain people wherever they met them, were much like our great Lincoln. Now we will go and see what this group is talking about. You must not laugh at the odd look of the teacher. He does not look like a Greek, for he is very ugly. His body is heavy and not at all a good shape, his nose is flat, and his eyes bulge out, and roll about in a very strange way. He is not at all well dressed, but these boys all seem to love him dearly; and after we listen a while and hear his fine lesson, showing that the beauty which springs from a well-trained mind is the greatest and truest beauty one can have, you forget how ugly he is, and wish you were an Athenian boy, and might come, when your lesson in the gymnasium is over, and talk to this wonderful man. Do you know the name of this great teacher? It is Socrates, the greatest philosopher of Greece. We must not think when we leave the gymnasium and go back to the city we shall not see Socrates again, for he is everywhere, from day to day,—in the streets or wherever he finds young men ready to listen and to talk about temperance, or play, or oratory, or eloquence, or any question about how to get most pleasure and profit out of life. He begins always by saying something that causes those who hear him to listen and think, and before they know it he has them taking a lively part in the discussion. As you cannot stay long in Athens, I will tell you, before we go on, what is to become of Socrates at last. It is very sad. He is never afraid to tell people when they are wrong; and he thinks many things men do are wrong, and tells them so. For this reason many people dislike him, and finally they say that he does not truly worship the Greek gods, and that he teaches the young men bad habits, because some of his pupils are very bad men. This is not because of what Socrates teaches them, but because they do not follow what he teaches. But the people do not believe this, and they say he must die. So they compel him to drink a cup of poison, and he takes it very bravely, with his sorrowing pupils about him, calmly teaching them to the very last how to live a true life in this world, and giving them some of the best reasons for believing in a life after death.

Where shall we go next? I wonder if you would not like to see where the laws of Athens are made. Come, then, let us see which way to go. We can always find the Acropolis, so let us start from there. We go about a quarter of a mile west, when we come to a large platform which has been built in an open square. It is called the Pnyx. Here all the citizens of Athens who are over eighteen years of age meet and pass laws for the city; for Athens is a democracy now, in Pericles' time, and all the people help to rule the little state. There is a meeting of the Assembly, as it is called, about forty times a year, or oftener, if it is needed. On Assembly days the citizens meet by daybreak, for the Athenians believe in getting up early. Sacrifices are offered to the gods first, then the omens are taken, and then business begins. Some man is leader, and he rules the meeting for that day. Socrates was often leader of the Assembly and often kept the people from doing hasty and wrong things. Any one has a right to talk in this meeting, only he must come out in front and stand on a large block of stone while he talks. This is called the "bema stone." Some one proposes something which he wants the people to do. Today they are to decide whether or not they shall pay the citizens who come to the Assembly to vote. Some are against it, saying that those who love their country should serve it without pay; others are for it, saying that only the rich people can afford to give their time. So the discussion goes on, each one as he speaks coming forward and mounting the bema stone. Finally Pericles comes forward to speak, and all are eager to hear. He speaks in favor of paying the citizens, not only for attending the Assembly, but also favors giving tickets to the theater to those who could not afford to buy them; for the theater to the Greek was a great source of education, and Pericles wished everybody to have an equal chance for education; so finally the vote is taken, and they decide to pay the citizens for serving on juries, attending the Assembly and the like, and also to give the people tickets to the theater. A government in which all the people come together like this and discuss matters and decide them is called a pure democracy. You notice they vote by holding up their hands,—that is one reason they never hold meetings after dark. They have no good way of lighting as we have. Did you know that the man who proposed the law they were discussing today was not just an ordinary member of the Assembly? He is what is called a Councilor. The Council is made up of five hundred men from the different tribes. These men meet every day and talk over laws, and the Assembly can vote only on the questions which the Council has already talked over. The man who ruled the Assembly was also appointed by the Council.

I told you the Council met every day. That is not quite right. Twice a year they have no meetings; those are the feast times of the year. One thing about these feast times you must see before you leave Athens.

We will go to the Acropolis again and pass around to the southwest side, and look at the great Greek theater. Does it not remind you of the way the amphitheater at the fair is built? But there is much difference; here the seats are steps cut in the rocky hillside, and are made of marble. They are arranged in a half-circle, and down on the level ground is what we would call the stage, where the singing and acting took place.

The Greeks did not go to the theater just to have a pleasant time, as we do. It was like going to church to them. They did it in honor of their gods. This one where we now are is built in honor of Dionysius, one of their gods. Men who write plays have them acted at these feast times, and there are judges to see which one is the best. Before daylight on feast days people begin coming to the theater to get good seats. The great people and officers and judges, have special seats. The people bring fruit and cakes along for lunch, for they expect to stay all day. The play begins, and everybody listens very closely. The actors do not have a very easy time unless they are very good, for if they so much as pronounce a word wrong, the people hiss at them and pelt them with figs and raisins. But if they are pleased, they show it just as plainly. After one part of a play is finished, the people rest a little, then another one begins, and so on all day long. Nearly every one in Athens is there: think what a large place this theater is! It would hold thirty thousand people. It is not easy for the actors to speak so as to be heard by so many people in the open air, and they use a kind of speaking trumpet to speak through; then they wear what they call masks, which are like false faces and cover their heads entirely. With these masks they can make themselves look like any one they choose. They are so far away from many of the people that they look very small, so they wear shoes with very thick soles and use a great many ways of making themselves look large. Some of the greatest Greek poets wrote plays to be acted in this theater; and we read and study today, the very plays these Greeks are going to see.

There are many more things it would delight us to see in Athens, but there is one thing you must yet see in Greece before we leave it.

In the southwestern part of Greece, near the shore of the sea, in a little river valley, is a place called Olympia, in the country of Elis, which every Greek knew about. Every fourth year, from all over Greece, people went to Olympia for the games. They came in the very hottest part of summer, in what we would call July or August, though the Greeks did not have those names for months. During the time of these games no Greek state could be at war with another, and Elis was to be protected by all. The roads that led to Olympia were repaired and made safe for travelers. You remember, at the time of the battles of Marathon and Thermopylæ, the Spartans would hardly send help because they were then holding their games. Like the plays at the theater, these games were in honor of a god. Those at Olympia were in honor of Zeus, the king of gods. There was no real town at Olympia, with hotels or places for the people to stay in, so the crowds lived in tents during the games. They came to Olympia from all over Greece, the islands of the Ægean, Asia Minor, Italy, everywhere that Greeks were to be found. They brought animals with them to sacrifice to the gods. Now we will imagine we have gone to the games. We are not the first ones there, for people whose friends are going to take part have been here a month or so already, and the people who are to be in the games have been here ten months already, practicing in the gymnasium at Olympia. On the eleventh day of the month the games begin. We must be on hand early if we get a place. It will be a long day, the sun is hot, and it is dusty. We must not wear hats, because it is not thought respectful to the gods to wear hats at these games. This first day sacrifices of oxen and sheep and goats are to be offered to the gods, and the people who are to take part are to draw lots, and thus decide when their time comes. Very little else will be done on this day. The second day the boys have their games, and run and wrestle and box and do many of the things they have been taught in the gymnasiums at home. But the third day is the great day, for then the men have their contests. They do about the same things that the boys did, only ever so much better. Thus the games continue for another day; then on the fifth day there will be many processions and feasts for the victors. Those who win are shown the highest possible honor, for to win in the Olympian games is thought to be the greatest thing a Greek can do. The winners are crowned with branches of olive, cut with a golden knife by a lad from the sacred wild-olive tree of Olympia, and palm branches are placed within their hands. They are then shown to the people while their names are proclaimed aloud by a herald, and their fathers' names also, and the country from which they come. When they go home, they are treated with the highest honor. A piece of the city wall is torn down, so they need not come in like common people, and to show that if all the citizens were as strong as the victor, the city would not need walls; their statues will be put up in the market place, and all the rest of their lives they will be treated with the greatest respect.

Do the Athenians ever work, you ask, or do they spend all their time in the gymnasiums, theater, and games? Well, the real Athenian does not do much work, for the work on the farms and in the city is done mostly by slaves. Greece did not have so many slaves at first in the time of Homer, or even when she was fighting her brave battles with Persia, and what slaves she did have had a pretty easy time; but in the time of Pericles there are perhaps ten slaves to every freeman, and the story of how they lived would be very sad indeed. The Athenian thinks it is his chief work to make the laws, write poems, carve statues, build temples, attend games and fight the battles of Athens, not to plow her fields or row her triremes.

Now our short visit to Athens is over, but we shall yet study about some of the great men of Greece in Pericles' time. We have seen her at the time when she was most beautiful, for before Pericles died a dreadful war broke out between Athens and Sparta, which lasted thirty years; and at the end of that time Athens was forced to tear down her walls, give up her ships, and was never again the ruler of Greece. But we have seen in this little visit many of the beautiful things which Athens made; and though Athens is soon overcome by other rulers, the sculpture and architecture and poetry and philosophy which she worked out so carefully and so wisely was not lost but spread out all over the Eastern world by Alexander. This we will presently study about; and finally in the fifth volume of this series, when we study the Renaissance, we shall see how all this beauty was carried westward into Europe. And we shall further see in the last volumehow we, in America, when we build a beautiful building, or place a statue in our homes, or in a public library, or museum, or schoolroom, or when we paint a beautiful picture, or write a fine poem, or make our own bodies straight and strong, and fit places for the growth of fine minds, that we have learned how to do very much of all this from these happy, free, art-loving Greeks. The little country of Greece did not teach as great a lesson of religion as the Jews taught, or trade over so much of the world as little Phoenicia, but they taught lessons of how to think and speak clearly, and how to carve, build and write so beautifully that the whole world still turns to Greece as its greatest teacher in these things.

The Story of Alexander the Great

WHAT do you think became of Athens, with all its beauty, which Pericles loved so well?

I will tell you. Just two years before Pericles died, that is, 431 years before Christ, Athens and Sparta and the other states of Greece began to fight each other as they often had done before, and for nearly a hundred years they quarreled most of the time. So many battles were fought that in the end all the states had become very weak and were without power, for they had lost a large number of their best men. Just then, for almost the first time, they began to hear of Macedonia.

Macedonia was a mountainous country about twice as far north of Athens as Sparta was southwest of it. Its people were Greeks, too, but in many ways they were not like the Greeks of Athens and Sparta.

Why had Macedonia not been heard of before? It was because its people still lived in country tribes and had not learned to live in cities. They did not have fine large temples for their gods until many years after the Athenians had. Great forests covered most of the country, and the people lived in rude houses and fed their few sheep on the mountain sides. They were fond of hunting, and often had to fight the wild beasts which came to steal away their sheep.

No boy could sit at the table with men until he had killed a wild boar, and every one that had not yet killed a foe must wear a rope around his body to show he was not yet free. Such wild life, and such struggles as these, made them brave and warlike, and they became most excellent fighters.

Once the Macedonians fought with Thebes and were overcome, and the people of Thebes made the king of Macedonia give them his little son Philip as a pledge that he would not trouble them again. While Philip was growing up at Thebes, he found out that the Greek cities were very jealous of each other, and kept fighting and trying to destroy each other.

When at last Philip's father died and Philip was allowed to go back home to be the king of Macedonia, he began to train his hardy, rough shepherds to fight. He taught them what he had learned at Thebes. He formed what was called a phalanx. Each soldier in the phalanx carried a light shield and a spear twenty one feet long. When they advanced, they were taught to place their shields together, somewhat like the scales on a fish, so as to form a wall, and they stood in rows, one behind another, sixteen men deep. Each soldier grasped the spear six feet from the front end, thrusting it forward just over the shoulders of those who stood before him; thus each man in the front row had four spears pointing before him.

Philip had seen how weak the Greek cities had become by their long wars, for they never learned to be true friends of one another; so he decided he would make war upon them, and in this way become ruler of all the Greeks.

Athens and Sparta and Thebes and all the rest of the Greek cities ceased quarreling for a little time, and united when they saw Philip coming; but in one great battle he defeated them all, and they were forced to choose him as their leader. So at last, you see, the Greek cities were no longer free, but all had become a part of Macedonia, and Philip was king over all of them.

Philip now asked them to join with him in making war on their old enemy Persia, who, you remember, had fought Greece, and burnt Athens to the ground about one hundred and fifty years before this time. He began to get his soldiers ready to start. Soon after this he was holding a great feast and games on his daughter's wedding day, and in the midst of the rejoicing he was murdered.

His son Alexander now became king. Alexander was only twenty years old, but he soon showed that he was even a greater king than his father had been. Two years before, when he was only eighteen, he had fought in the great battle in which the Macedonians had overcome the other Greeks, and his father had praised him for his bravery.

When he was thirteen, a beautiful but wild and fiery horse was brought to his father's court. None of the king's men could manage it, so King Philip had ordered them to take it away, when Alexander said, "I could manage that horse better than those men do." Philip, hearing him say it, let him try. Alexander saw the horse was afraid of its shadow. So he turned the horse directly toward the sun, in order that it might not see the shadow. He stroked it gently, and soon it became very quiet. Then he gave a quick leap and was on the horse's back. At first it tried to throw him off, but Alexander managed it so well that soon he was riding about as if it were an old and gentle horse. He was very fond of it, and named it Bucephalus. In later years Bucephalus carried him safely through many battles, and at last, when the faithful animal became old and died, Alexander built a city and named it Bucephalia.

Alexander was not only brave, but he was also studious. His father got for him the best teachers that could be found. He sent for Aristotle, the wisest man in all Greece. The boy loved Aristotle and studied hard. He thought there was nothing too hard for him to learn, but he liked the "Iliad" best of all, for it told of wars and the old Trojan and Greek heroes. It is said he knew it all by heart.

While he was yet a boy, the king of Persia sent some men to Philip on a matter of business, but Philip did not happen to be at home. So Alexander had to entertain the men. Although a boy, he surprised them by the intelligent questions he asked about Persia. He wanted to know how far they had come, and if the roads were good; how large was the king's army, and whether the people liked him, and many other things like these.

Once, when he heard that his father had captured another city, he said to his playmates, "My father will go on until he has conquered all the cities, and there will be none left for us to take when I am king."

But as I have said, Philip was killed when Alexander was only twenty. Alexander soon showed that he could manage a state as well as he had managed Bucephalus. Because he was so young, the Greeks whom his father had conquered thought they could easily win back their freedom. But Alexander marched swiftly from one end of his kingdom to the other, overcoming them everywhere, and soon things were quiet again. Then he decided to take up his father's plan of conquering Persia.

Very soon he had gathered an army of about thirty thousand and was ready to start. Soon they had reached the Hellespont and were ready to cross into Asia. Here is where Xerxes had crossed into Europe on his bridge of boats one hundred and fifty years before, when he came with a million men to conquer Greece. Alexander is now crossing to conquer Persia.

But can he do it? Persia is fifty times as large as Macedonia, including all Greece, and has an army more than twenty times as large as Alexander's. But you remember the Macedonian phalanx. We are now to see if a small army with a brave leader like Alexander is more powerful than a large army with a poor leader like Darius, the king of Persia.

Soon they crossed the Hellespont. Alexander himself guided one of the vessels, and when they came near the shore he hurled his spear into the bank, to show his men how he aimed to conquer Persia. He was the first one to jump ashore; and how he must have felt, for now he was in the land of Troy,—the land of the hero Achilles, the warrior whom he had worshiped from childhood, and whom he loved to think he was like,—the land of Paris and Helen and old King Priam, the heroes of whom Homer had sung.

He went to the spot where the proud city of Troy had stood so long ago. He found the places where it was said Achilles had fought and where he lay buried. In order to show him honor,

Alexander told his men to celebrate the games. So all the warriors put aside, for a few days, thoughts of war and danger, and enjoyed themselves as they used to do in the gymnasium at home. Through all the years of marching and fighting Alexander never forgot the games his soldiers knew and loved, and often they laid aside the dangers of war, and by hunting, the theater, and the gymnastic sports, enjoyed themselves in the camp. But Alexander did more than this, for he ordered a new city to be built where Troy had once stood, and he named it Ilium in honor of the old city and his most treasured book, the "Iliad."

Alexander longed to fight as the ancient Greeks at Troy had fought. He wanted to win a glorious victory. His wishes were soon to be granted, for he had not gone far eastward when he came to the Granicus River, in Asia Minor, where the Persian army was placed, so that he must drive them away if he wished to cross.

The Macedonian king did not hesitate. He mounted his horse and asked the men to remember how well they had fought for his father. The command was given for the battle to begin, when on they went, through the valley and river, singing the battle hymn. Alexander was in the thickest of the fight. His lance was broken. He was hit on the head by a sword, and a piece of his helmet was broken. He would certainly have been killed, had not his friend Clitus rushed to his aid and saved his life. In spite of the size of the Persian army, he completely scattered all of it and won a great victory. By one battle he had freed all of the Greek cities in Asia Minor.

Marching on, Alexander came to the city of Gordium, once the home of greedy, rich King Midas, who wanted everything he touched to be turned to gold. In a temple the people showed him a wagon to which the yoke was fastened by a knotted cord, and they told him that whoever would untie it should become ruler of all Asia. Alexander tried to unfasten it as many others had done; but when he found it was very difficult, he drew his sword and cut the string, and so it came off.

Soon he reached the Issus River, near the northeast angle of the Mediterranean Sea, and found out that Darius himself was coming with a large army to fight him. This is just what Alexander wanted.

What a splendid sight the Persian army made as it marched along! First came the silver altar, bearing the sacred fire; then came youths, one for each day in the year, in front of the chariot of the sun, drawn by white horses. On the chariot sat the king, wearing a fine purple mantle, containing many precious stones. Around him on every side were his soldiers, many of them wearing robes glittering with gold and carrying silver-handled lances.

Then they began to fight. The battle was sharp and Alexander was wounded; but as usual he won the victory. Darius soon saw that the Persians were beaten, so he jumped on a horse and hurried away to escape with his life, leaving behind his wife, his mother and children, as well as his purple mantle. But Alexander was not cruel to his fair prisoners, and Darius' own mother said she was treated better by her kingly captor than she had been by Darius himself.

That night Alexander ate the supper which had been prepared for Darius, and slept in Darius' tent. He and his plain Macedonian soldiers were surprised at the many fine things they had captured. There were dishes and pitchers and bath-tubs of solid gold, won drously made. The odors of spices and myrrh sweetened the king's tent. Fine carpets and rugs were there in great abundance; and, what pleased the soldiers greatly, they found a large pile of Persian money.

The Greeks now entered Phoenicia, the land where stood the city of Tyre. You remember that earlier you learned how the merchants from Tyre sailed over all the seas trading with the different countries, carrying the goods from one place to another. In this way the people became very rich and proud and had built around the edge of their island-city a wall one hundred and fifty feet high, made out of large stones, accurately joined and tightly cemented. On the shore, a half mile away, stood the old city. They thought they would be forever safe behind the walls of their new city; and well they might, for once Nebuchadnezzar of Babylon, with a great army, had tried thirteen years to capture it and had failed. But Nebuchadnezzar was not an Alexander.

The Tyrians did not wish the Greek army to enter their city, so they left all the houses on the shore in the old town and shut themselves behind the great walls on the island-city. Alexander had no fear that he would not be able to capture it, but how was he to get over the half mile of water which extended between the coast and the city?

He decided to build a road out through the water to the island. So he tore down the houses on the shore and brought down trees from Mt. Lebanon near by, and tumbled rocks, wood, dirt and all— a whole forest and a whole city—into the sea, making a path two hundred feet wide, reaching from the shore to the walls. The Tyrians tried to tear up the way, but the Greek soldiers quickly repaired it every time it was torn down.

But how will the Greeks break down the walls when they get to them? Will they use cannon to break them to pieces, as we would? No, indeed, they will not; for in that day, and for almost two thousand years afterward, there were no cannon, and gunpowder was not known.

They tried to dig holes under the sides of the wall so as to cause it to fall, but the Tyrians threw down stones and poured kettles of hot oil upon the men who were digging and drove them away. Then the soldiers built huge battering-rams with which to batter the walls to pieces. A battering-ram is a large pole, thicker and longer than the largest telegraph pole, the end of which is covered with a head of hard iron. The pole is hung on a chain in a frame, so it may be moved back and forth lengthwise, heavily battering against the solid wall. Day after day for seven long months they beat at the strong walls and hurled immense stones and sharp bars of iron at them with another machine, called a catapult, till at last they broke through a hole large enough for some of the soldiers to enter. Alexander was one of the first inside, and soon the city was captured. What do you think became of the people? Well, some of them were killed, but most of them were sold as slaves, and some of them were cruelly crucified. Thus the city of Tyre completely lost the importance which it had so long held as the queen city of the eastern Mediterranean. After Tyre is destroyed, there is for fifty years or more no great city on the eastern Mediterranean coast.

Alexander next went to Egypt, and the people there who were tired of being ruled by Persia gladly welcomed him. He spent the winter there and started a city at the place where the Nile empties into the blue Mediterranean. He named this Alexandria, after himself, just as we named our capital after Washington, our first president. He divided the city into three main parts, one for the Greeks, one for the Hebrews, and one for the Egyptians, but he wanted all nations of people to come there to live. I will tell you more of Alexandria by and by, but now I must finish about Alexander's great conquests.

When spring came, Alexander again set out, for he had not yet come to the Persian capital. Eastward he went over rivers and hills, through green valleys, and then over hot burning deserts. King Darius, after running away in the last battle, had by this time collected another large army,—larger than the one before. This time, besides the enormous army of soldiers, he had more than two hundred war chariots with sharp swords and scythe blades fastened to the end of the tongue, and to the ends of the axle. He expected to mow down Alexander's army as a farmer would cut his grass and wheat.

Alexander came up with him near the town of Arbela, in the rich valley of the Tigris, and fought here his third and last great battle with him; but like the others, Alexander won it. King Darius again escaped, but Alexander now entered the capitals of Babylon, Susa and Persepolis. Here he found the hoarded wealth of the king, and great it surely was, for it took five thousand camels and a whole host of mules to carry away the treasure. Some of it he sent back to Greece, and the rest he kept for his own use and to divide among his soldiers.

He had now really gone as far as he at first intended, but, you see, he had not yet taken Darius. So allowing all his soldiers who cared to do so to go back home, where they would tell of the riches they had found and thus induce others to come to help him, and leaving men to take care of the captured cities, he again started after Darius. Many days he followed him. Sometimes he was almost up with him, but still Darius kept ahead. At last Darius' own men saw it was of no use to try longer to escape, so they tried to kill the king to keep him from being captured; and when Alexander at last overtook him, he was dying. Sorry to see him treated so cruelly, Alexander ordered the body to be taken back to the capital, and there buried in the beautiful tomb of the Persian kings.

Now that Darius was dead, Alexander called himself king of Persia and began to dress and act something like the Persian kings. His plain Macedonian soldiers did not like this, but Alexander thought by doing so, it would be the best way to unite the Persians with the Greeks, so that he might truly rule over both.

Still Alexander went on. He fought many fierce, brave battles with tribes in Central Asia, and overcame them all. That he might easily hold all the country, wherever he went he built cities something like Alexandria, and left in them some of his soldiers who no longer cared to fight, or were worn out by the long marches. Many traders also who followed the army to sell their goods to the soldiers, saw that they could profitably remain to supply the people with what they needed. Some of the natives, too, were brought from the country and from little villages and placed in the cities.

In this way more than seventy cities were built, and you may be sure these Greek cities grew to be very much like those at home. The people spoke the Greek language and had their gymnasia, Greek sports, theaters and temples. They remembered their Homer and taught others to know it, and in their theaters they gave the plays of Æschylus, which had so often delighted the Athenians when Pericles lived. Do you begin to see how Alexander made Persia like Greece? And also how he was spreading over the old worn-out East a layer of rich soil of Greek beauty as farmers sometimes spread a fertilizer over their worn-out fields?

Do you think Alexander had forgotten his old teacher, Aristotle? No, indeed, he had not, for wherever he went he had many men to find out all they could about the people they met and the countries through which they passed, so they might send back this knowledge to Aristotle. He set many men to work also to gather all the different kinds of plants from mountain sides and woods and fields and deserts, and these he sent back to Aristotle, that he might study them. Alexander, too, furnished the great teacher of his boyhood all the money he needed in his work, and so made it possible for him to study and teach in Athens. Aristotle was one of the greatest men who ever lived, and by his study and writing people now know many things about Greece and the olden times which they never would have known had it not been for him.

But Alexander was not always so good as you might think, for he loved to have his men gather at his royal tent to drink wine with him, and sometimes he would even get drunk. Once, when he had drunk too much wine, he became very angry at his best friend, Clitus, who, you remember, had saved his life at the battle of the Granicus River. Before Alexander thought what he was doing, he threw his spear at Clitus and killed him. He was very sorry for his act and shut himself in his tent and would not see any one for many days. You surely think this should have taught him to let wine alone, but I am sorry to say it did not.

Alexander, still traveled eastward, coming at last to the Indus River, where a branch of the early Aryan people lived. His soldiers did not wish to go farther, so they begged him to return to Babylon, for it was now ten years since they had left Macedonia.

Alexander still wished to make Persia and Greece more like each other in customs and life, so he married the beautiful daughter of Darius and urged his Greek soldiers to marry Persian women also. Many did so, and they made a great wedding feast, which lasted five whole days. Thousands of Greeks and Persians were present to enjoy this feast—made rich with the wealth and luxury of Persia and beautiful with the art and culture of Greece. It was held in a great hall decorated in most expensive style. Elegant couches for those who dined to recline upon, costly Persian rugs, hangings of fine linen, tapestries of many colors interwoven with threads of gold, pillars overlaid with silver and gold, and precious jewels, tell us that this Alexander is quite different from the plain, simple, manly Macedonian king and soldier who had crossed the Hellespont only ten years before.

But in spite of his many successes, Alexander was not nearly so happy as he used to be when he was king of only little Macedon. He no longer had the fine health which had so often helped him to brave hardships, for he had become weakened by eating and drinking too much, and returning to Babylon, where he feasted much, it was not long until he became very sick.

The doctors crowded around his bed and did their best to save his life, but they soon saw that he must die. When the soldiers found this out, they were wild with grief and all wanted to see their loved leader once again. Silently and sadly they passed by his bedside and looked on his dying face, which they had so often seen bright and full of joy. It was sad that Alexander should die so young, for he was only thirty-three, and had just begun his great work of spreading Greek culture over the then known world and of uniting the many different people whom he had conquered.

Alexander had many faults, but the people loved him, for he really tried to do very much to help them. Both by war and by sowing broadcast the seeds of Greek life, he had well earned the title of Alexander *the Great.*

When Alexander died, his body was embalmed, laid in a golden coffin and taken, as is generally believed, to the city of Alexandria, where a fine tomb was built for it. And this brings us back to the wonderful city founded but a few years before at the mouth of the Nile. Alexandria grew very rapidly, and soon became the most important city in the world. Since Tyre was destroyed, the traders of the Mediterranean Sea must find a new city as a center, and it was to take the place of Tyre that Alexandria was built. It had such a fine harbor that ships from all countries came there to trade. Athens sent ships to get the grain from the Nile valley; camels brought ivory and lions' skins from southern Egypt; from Arabia and far-away India the caravans brought costly gems and spices; ships came with loads of furs and fish from the Baltic Sea; Spain sent its large amount of precious silver. As a spider sits at the center of its web catching food in its meshes from every direction, so Alexandria sat as the mistress of the Mediterranean, drawing trade from every quarter east and west.

Thus it was not long until Alexandria was doing the trading for most of the world and was even a greater city than Tyre had ever been. She was the halfway point between the rich and luxurious peoples living in the Indus and Tigro-Euphrates valleys in the Old East and the youthful peoples growing up on the western shores of the Mediterranean and on the western coast of Europe. I must briefly tell you something more about this greatest of all the cities founded by Alexander.

The governor of Egypt, who was one of Alexander's own Greek generals, built for himself a fine marble palace in the center of the city. Most of the people spoke the Greek language and learned the Greek ways. Soon they had a theater for the Greek plays and a gymnasium for the games. Near his palace the governor built a large library. He sent men to Athens and the other Greek cities to get copies of all their books. Others were sent to copy the clay bricks of Babylon. The Jews brought the Hebrew Bible which they loved so much, and it, too, was changed to Greek.

As we found in studying Egypt and bookmaking last year, the books were written on a kind of paper which they called papyrus. This was made from the thin coats of a reed-like plant which grew in Egypt. After the paper was made, strips of it were cut just as wide as a book was to be, and then a number of wide strips were glued end to end, thus making a strip of paper from eight to fourteen inches wide and just as long as was desired, fifty or a hundred feet, or even sometimes much longer. The pages were written down the sheets. On each end of the paper a stick, usually with fine knobs, was fastened, and on one of these sticks the whole was rolled, somewhat as we roll a map. When one wanted to read the book, he unrolled it from one stick to the other as he read. Each of these rolls came to be called a volume, for that was the ancient word for a roll; and you see we have kept the idea of books being rolls to this day, for we still call them volumes. So the work went on, and so eager was the governor to get a copy of every book for the library, it is said he even ordered persons to steal books in the various countries if they could not get them any other way. The library grew to be very large, and we are told that at one time it had more than seven hundred thousand volumes. How strange this library of papyrus rolls would have seemed to us; but we should be glad all this was done, for, by gathering so much of the learning together in one place, and by changing much of the old writing into the Greek, it made it much easier for many scholars to learn it, and hand it down, to all after ages, even to our own time.

The governor, too, built a large building, in which he gathered all the kinds of plants which could be found, and in another he placed a large collection of wild animals. Then he sent for the wisest men to study the books, the plants and the animals. From everywhere they came,—from Athens, from Babylon, from Jerusalem and from far-away Sicily and India. In order that they need not stay away if they were poor, he built large buildings in which they might live, and furnished them with board. It is said that at one time more than fourteen thousand people were there to study. What a fine school that must have been, in those olden days!

Thus you see that while many people in that far-away time were interested mostly in war and such things, yet some people were beginning to be great scholars, and gathered together the best that had been thought and said all over the world, and wrote it out in their own language. By this means they preserved learning and made it so that they and their people could better understand it, and not only teach it to their children, but add a few new thoughts to it, and their children in turn to their children, in this way making knowledge like a river which grows continually wider and deeper by the streams which flow into it. It is by work like this that knowledge has grown "from more to more," as Tennyson says.

Thus I hope you see that Alexander was not chiefly a rude warrior, selfishly overturning cities and countries, but he was more like a missionary who carries new thought to a people and thus lifts them to a higher life. Athens was not to have all of its art, its Homer, its Æschylus and its many other great things longer to itself, but they flowed out from Greece over Asia and Egypt, and some were left wherever Alexander's work extended. This out-pouring of Greece was much like the Nile River overflowing its banks and spreading out over the country, bringing moisture and fertile soil to every part of the valley. So Alexander's going out over the borders of little Greece caused the streams of beauty and truth, as sculpture and architecture and poetry and philosophy, which had become stagnant, to flow over and enrich the people of the old East. Thus Greece was able to pay back those old countries for the help they had given her, by giving her ideas and useful things, when she was a mere infant—just getting a start. Inthe study of Rome we shall see Greek life and art carried west and spread over the western Mediterranean; and as we study later we shall see how it goes on to Western Europe, and how finally its influence will be seen reaching out to every American home which has in it artistic mantle-pieces, or wall-paper, or linoleum, or beautiful patterns for chair or piano, or plate or picture. Thus the beautiful and true things which Greece worked out were not permitted to remain in that little country, but have been spread over much of the world to give it a taste for simple grace and artistic life.

69749123R00033

Made in the USA
Middletown, DE
21 September 2019